Pas d'affiches
Lary Timewell
Obvious Epiphanies Press
Copyright 2011
All rights reserved.
Cataloging information:
ISBN 978-1-105-03818-1

Pas d'affiches

Lary Timewell

Polaroid SX-70's
of street posters
Paris, Montreal, Vancouver
1986 - 1988

obvious epiphanies press
japan

- for Lorraine Gilbert

Once & The

Plots fragment
    where subtitles fail
    I can't believe my eyes
    fall into old habits of
    document   head sense
    once appeared bold
    the vertical juxtaposition
    the linear like a cross
    obliterates always   the
    text giving up
    credit where music's due
    yet these eyes believe
    the   the   the
    stuttering film of the text
    which once itself appeared
    red   a sexual revolution   just
    whose face of last year's media
    a made   a manipulative
    intention of dramatic musical
           scores
    not produced so much as
    let loose from the eyes have it
    now habit   of deconstruction
    written & realized long
    after Cezanne   I'm
           glad Gertrude
           saw her chance
           when she did
           what she did

Rien & Creation

Harvest moon in ragtime
    torn from its tough

        & pliant sense, sweet blue
        jellyroll of season

        slides into the sea
        of an old Orleans, shrill

        carnival
        accordion of agreement

        The notes' noisy tinman
        dance builds up

        jazz around in
        middle C,

        a chemical festival
        as burst from barbed wire

        the all or nothing of this of
        any song's necessity

        : the axe fell square
        followed   in time

        by the tree

Cafe & Vogue

Roll your own in accents
acute, savour that saviour protein, that
radio readymade. Give name to it

& then... what? L.H.O.O.Q.? Graphic
immanence & kinetic destination.

To affix, with the lips, a stylus to a tree burl.

No less the ochre of autumn than an abrasive
blanket stuffed into a busted amp. The smears

of impenetrable perfection, an animal called
perhaps to keep you warm in winter. At home

& homeless on Rue St. Laurent, guarding tape
transcriptions of Gregorian chant, liturgical

odors & fleshy artifice,
enfolded in the open field.

Cosmos & October Tent

It begins decomposing
    beauty

    calls rust out from under
    the layers of language unglued

    curved watermarks of
    time collecting

    alms for the trust
    fund of meaning

    as from a forest
    step these syllables

    rain on the canvas versus
    keys of the clavier stuck

    c/osmosis   absorbed in
    reading under a blanket of pulp

    autumns spring one-liners
    on the audience our eyes

    resiliant nation a flesh
    yet fears to be undone

    by assembly & gathering
    timely promotional scrap/s

    thin banner flaps
    in the wind
    ing wind

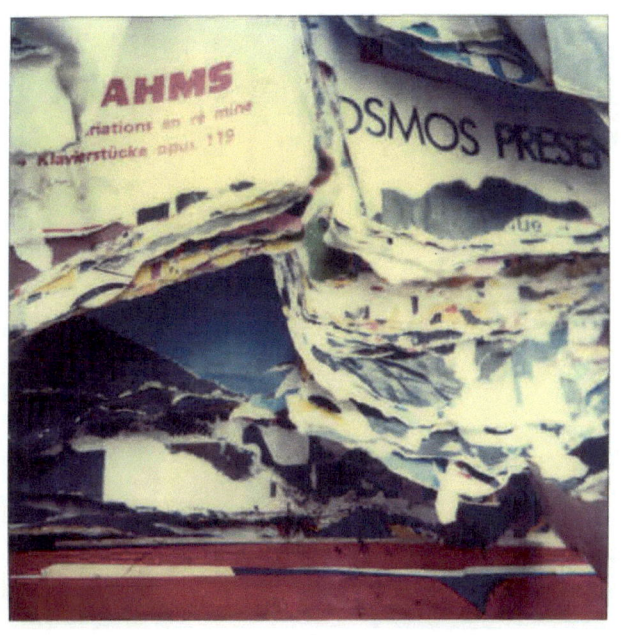

La Mort & Le Party Fou

A spear taunts the edge
    of our limited nuclear

    vision of ourselves
    holding guns to the head

    the heart has
    barely enough

    time to make
    a little o in death o

    don't go out in the woods today
    it's sure to be a surprise

    it's bears & eagles & Candu geese
    dancing mayday

    from pole to frozen pole a mad
    house on fire

    a superpowered party

    come as you were
    an instant ago

Votre Liberté & Space Flowers

Headlines shred your sleep
    leave you only this
    undersurface of waking to
    anxiety   fatigue
    a vague resistance
    memories of *film noir* fade
    gesture across generation
    reduced by   replaced by
    a logical fiscal language
    entropic computerese

    founding father wisdom
    decrees   now this
    is for your own good   could
    hurt us more than
    it's going to hurt you
    to agree   say *oui*
    say *ja*   say *da da*

    et déchirez les affiches

    your alphabet
    has cornered you
    cubist Castro-lover
    Star Wars is just
    this year's Peter Pan
    & space junk flowers
    in the O zone of
    your dream of
    intelligent life
                out there

Chi

In the stream of all this taking
    tiger mountain by storm

no sense of a banner
that is not music

for the spirit
any of us could be

dancer among this paper
prayer tied to ancestral trees

in the year of the ox
in the tugging of the heart

the East
is read is

shaped kite of hyperbole
after all

Misogynème & Victor Men

Fetch says the fire-eater
    in his best master's voice
    lay that newsprint at my feet
    he's the adverse emblazoned
    bold-faced type
    guard to this planetary
    & household
    pet behind bars
    a sidekick to bare her teeth
    he tosses off another floral
    Molotov description
    40's private dick
    dime novel in the hip
    streetsmart readership
    a heckler at poetry's side-
    show something always
    inflammable on his breath
    in the fade of the latest
    thru hoops of fire &
    floodlights of publicity
    no accident but how we're taught
    another trick for attention
    in obedience school
    a nicely packaged letter-bomb
    a howling inside out

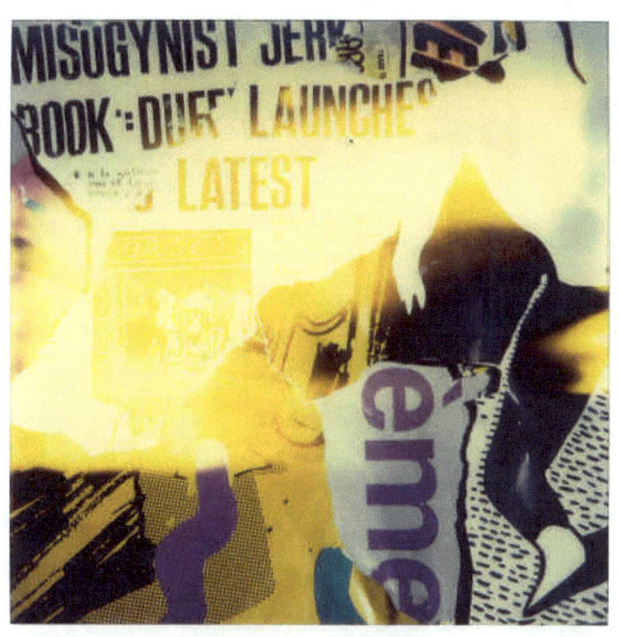

Open City & Pink Megaphone

It's all about surveillance
    my love says

    this one shocks   crows
    like mirrors   all about

    getting your attention first
    then moving in for

    the fixing of sights on selling
    how her & it get identified

    sign profit in
    solid masculine metric

    shivering cheerleaders
    on the sidelines instructed

    what to how to
    urge on the team

    a blast signals open
    season on her

    implicit & anonymous
    image as carnival queen

    I sense more than see
    a green ape looking in

    the pool startled by
    my hand in it

Geronimo & Silence

Map of the New World where
essence credo dwelt. What

is the aesthetic life of earth?
Amorphous marble of waves

more rhythmic in the Gulf of Mexico.
Passage to India, *our* Amerigo Vespucci

making fertile an all-pervasive art
& selling it wholesale. Components

from Europe ghostdance in an afterlife of
attitudes, a shrinking Amazon of memory.

Invisible bird in coppered light; resonance
not resemblance. An opaque theology

of destiny made manifest. Colour turns
to presence from anywhere we watch

deep inside
a private politic, a *camera
oscura.*

Banner & Lock-out

A ny similarity between a loaf of bread
& a book is but an unintended march

    across the steppes of murky how.
    Commodity malpractice of the masses.

    Whistle-blowers as security risks. Rote,
    concussed versions of natural speech.

    Traditional *kitsch* has the taste of *quiche*,
    the look of pre-urban bird-watching.

    In the accelerated destabilization of object
    capitalism, the dogma posits an outcry.

    Words in
    other words,

    the old

    as above,
    so below.

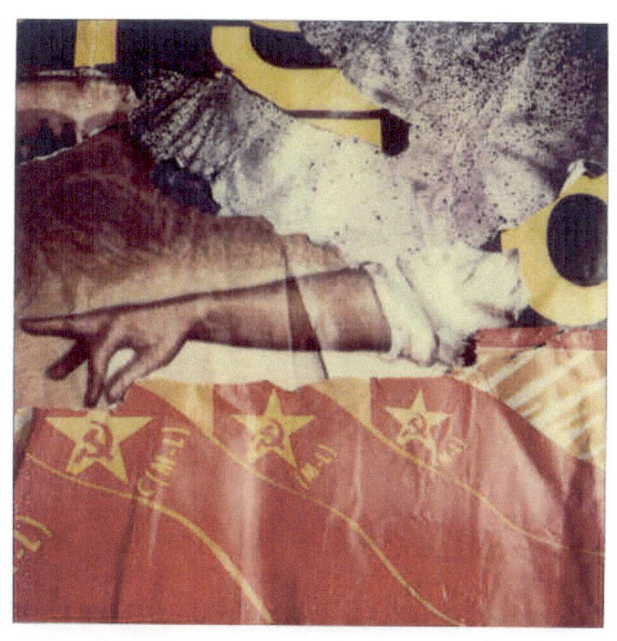

Fou-fou & Les vestiges d'amour

You grip hard & hold on tight, take a swing
lick at colour, but the message turns out
to be a grocery list.

        All the vitamins of
        hormonal aura flood
        light, undermine each
        autobiographical
        amen.

In the arbitrary buzz
of the schoolyard, more randomness
than an opera of meadow, more of
the ragged sleep continues
under dream.

        Oddity arrangement :
      the dragonfly & the hydro-electric
      typesetter, both captives torn
        from sanctuary.

Local love
remains the staple, remains
intact, &

     for each verb that meets the brain,
    an arc of music comes from over the hill.
        a tonic of rain.

Somewhere between
the durge & the daydream, this ability
to mutter with the hands.

Marx & Your Babies Grow

Look no farther for the advent of
appalling acts for political ends.

here again, we commemorate
anachronistic nature. All very

nice as a rhythm of concerns, but an
argument elegant malice does not make.

The words merely serve as spatial
proletarians in bunny slippers.

As an impetuous forward rush
which degenerates into "art".

Vernissage / métier / fête, shot
belly-level with colonial detachment.

The point of focus is never one, is never
the definitive accord of perception, is

a mid-view askew, adjacent to
the classical, the historical.

Class struggles

first to its knees.

La Ultima Hora

Celluloid sky, come to this one as
one poorly understood.

Photography pleases
like a mug of bees.

Circumstantial space,
a sheet of plastic.

persona non grata

Cancelled by law, by
gradations of light.

Perpetual sliding of
complicated surfaces.

Words, large islands of
windows & bars;

last chance to
dance figures.

From each tactile point we
peel the darkness back.

Cabana & Red Serif

Shadows & light
.
.
.
.
.
.

run down the wall
to residue

coral pink &
turquoise blue.

Text is the hero of sadness & border disputes
& milky sandals & salmon-pink bedspreads.

Distant sky, all
sky-blue & *soi-disant*.

Somewhere out there,
      simultaneous

         fonts of feeling,
         figures of power.

Bomb Brulait & Tribal Drum

Teaming with subliminals, libidinal
stuff, electrofunk, neither
pastiche nor personal
document of invention,
loving recidivist rock,
just when it seemed safe
to alter the ego of such
anthemic substance abuse,

& aside from the brooding
gravitus & snazzy buzz of
deadpan fez, delivery is stark
even by the blank standards
of post-whimper tweedy
aftermath facsimile fidgets,
sufferhead sermons, good
times you've never had,
fluorescent melodies you
never wanted, music

Oppenheimer
never knew.

Poste Canada & Modern Space

Constructivist crafted maple interiors
ของ the letter. A shop steward's

mosaic of millenial leftovers,
or an elegant implication

reduced to numerology. Heart-
beat elevated to a similacrum of

emotion, each of us responding
with an *animated* detachment,

absorbing whole entities
through the auditory canal.

Colliding habits build an over-sized
outcome. Apostrophes of gesture say

'the answer' is here, here in a source
boredom called method.

Burnished & Red

B ook burning for the urgent
enlightenment of youth.

The history of painting
the painting of history.

Blacktopped, even as to
tar the shadows.

The damp engine of *contralto*,
an alto sax on blocks.

Musky madrona, arcane
& Byzantine envy.

Singing scales. Singing

the leafy curvature of
a gothic subversion.

Full to bursting

Smithrite below my window
with a topping of foam.

Walk these sepulchral chutes,
soundlessly in snow.

Breton & La Poupée

> *"Man, that inveterate dreamer, daily more discontent with his destiny, has trouble assessing the objects he has been led to use."*

Angel wings & the counter-clockwise effects of an acidic

rain, until the map looks nothing like the thicket.

The wall calendar curls over the eternal month, over

the virtuosity -- the golden viscosity -- of accident.

These cilia filaments of inner ear are the recording angel.

The mind is made of symbols & minuscule footnotes.

The mind is made of paraphernalia piled on pool tables,

& the meaning (meaning) can barely withstand the music.

Meaning wings o'er the TV-flecked tundra. All meaning is

contradiction, all meaning is other : *Le rêve est féminin.*

Le Vent du nord & En direct

Take two, a view of multiple ancillary glyphs,
each soloing in the field. Reagan's

banality over a technical apparatus
called Mu. The content of nothingness

(the cult of *kawaii*) rejects any notion
of *the antecedent real*. Return to

the immediacy of direct experience

*"by refusing to accept a retrospective
reconstruction of reality"*

Not static / not reified
(stale) / (refried)

Not tender abstraction nor
what one willfully thinks…

more like *Euphony, you phony!*
disco songs for radio ads

More more more &
How do you like it

remembering I'm With Stupid
T-shirts

Ahére & Illusory Desire

Wrought iron rococo, sunlit balcony
of mid-day. The ideologies

    are mad, but the heart is open.
    Whirling footwork embroiders

    song as a layering of semantic
    expectations. Across vertiginous

    revelations & clefts of danger
    roams the aggregate hunger.

    An epistolomaniacal replacement-
    symphony slathered with agnostic

    marmalade, the words themselves
    the croissants & poltergeists that

    by evening
    I understand.

Dennis Brown & Youth Culture

L eafy aloe vera crossing petrochemical fjords
in pituitary harmony. Serrated cadence

    guiding. Absorbent sweep of crepuscular
    orchard. Grazing goats, cloudless azure,

    glandular lakes. An epic exquisite in its
    bioluminescence. Zephyr replicants

    in their muu-muus and *espadrilles*. Last
    purple prose for the teleprompter baby.

Your Mother Wears & Bootsy Bass

Pockets of orchestral cosmic trump-up,
mothership synth, Tuvan
throat singer in a blender,
ersatz croon over organ fills,
hypnotic cloisters of conical splice,
yelping pup auteur elude,
baroque landscape in shadow portal,
& the hung-over ambience of all that
cloaked-in-the allegorical
breaking of bread.

Versus.

Dumb punks nailed it:
3 chords & the truth

Endpiece

These SX-70 Polaroids were taken between 1986 and 1988 on the streets of Paris, Vancouver, & Montreal, and were subsequently used as springboards to writing. The resultant poems were among my first attempts at exploring language operations on the level of semiotic resonance (or less pretentiously put, a visio-linguistic echo or transference) rather than produce writing of a more directly confessional or entirely referential nature. As I see them now, the earlier poems, at the front of the book, seem fraught with 'message' and almost attempt narrative, while the somewhat later poems take far many more associative risks & leaps. Despite the *Pas d'affiches* prohibition, it was an era of rampant postering in all three cities, and the weather-ravaged build-up of pulpy colour was a daily visual attraction for me. More importantly, the uncontrolled & random washed-out effects of the SX-70 camera (so 'chemical', so 'filmy' and pre-digital) seemed just right to my low-fidelity sensibilities. Eight black and white diptych sets of these photographs, with their accompanying texts, were published in The Capilano Review, Issue #41, 1986.

Lary Timewell,
Sept. 2011,
Koriyama.

oep